W9-BQU-633

Landform Top Tens

The World's Most Amazing Islands

Anita Ganeri

Chicago, Illinois

www.heinemannraintree.com
Visit our website to find out more information about Heinemann-Raintree books.

To order:
☎ Phone 888-454-2279
▭ Visit www.heinemannraintree.com to browse our catalog and order online.

Edited by Louise Galpine, Kate DeVilliers, and Rachel Howells
Designed by Victoria Bevan and Geoff Ward
Original illustrations © Capstone Global Library Limited
Illustrated by Geoff Ward
Picture research by Hannah Taylor
Production by Alison Parsons

Printed and bound in China by CTPS

13 12 11 10 09
10 9 8 7 6 5 4 3 2 1

Library of Congress Cataloging-in-Publication Data

Ganeri, Anita, 1961-
  The world's most amazing islands / Anita Ganeri.
    p. cm. -- (Landform top tens)
  Includes bibliographical references and index.
  ISBN 978-1-4109-3700-1 (hc) -- ISBN 978-1-4109-3708-7 (pb)
  1. Islands--Juvenile literature. I. Title.
  GB471.G36 2008
  551.42--dc22
                                        2008051494

Acknowledgments

We would like to thank the following for permission to reproduce photographs: Alamy pp. 22 (Daniel and Flossie White), 27 (Thorsten Eckert); Ardea.com pp. 16 (Steffen and Alexandra Sailer), 17 (Dae Sasitorn), 18 (Bob Gibbons), 24 (Stefan Meyers); Corbis p. 20 (Frans Lanting); FLPA pp. 7 (Minden Pictures/ Tui De Roy), 9 (Minden Pictures), 11 (Frans Lanting), 13 (Minden Pictures/ Pete Oxford), 21 (Frans Lanting), 26 (imagebroker / Josef Beck); Lonely Planet p. 8 (Karl Lehmann); naturepl p. 25 (Pete Oxford); Photolibrary pp. 5 (Flirt Collection/ Jim Zuckerman), 6 (Mauritius/ Trond Hillestad), 10 (Purestock), 14 (Hemis/ John Frumm), 23 (Nordic Photos/ Chad Ehlers); Robert Harding p. 12; Science Photo Library p. 19 (Jeremy Walker); Still Pictures p. 15 (Mike Kolloffel).

Background images by Photodisc.

Cover photograph of Bora Bora Island in French Polynesia, reproduced with permission of Photolibrary (Nordic Photos/ Chad Ehlers).

We would like to thank Nick Lapthorn for his invaluable help in the preparation of this book.

Every effort has been made to contact copyright holders of material reproduced in this book. Any omissions will be rectified in subsequent printings if notice is given to the publishers.

Disclaimer

All the Internet addresses (URLs) given in this book were valid at the time of going to press. However, due to the dynamic nature of the Internet, some addresses may have changed, or sites may have changed or ceased to exist since publication. While the author and publishers regret any inconvenience this may cause readers, no responsibility for any such changes can be accepted by either the author or the publishers. It is recommended that adults supervise children on the Internet.

Contents

Some words are printed in bold, **like this**. You can find out what they mean by looking in the glossary on page 31.

Islands

An island is a piece of land that is completely surrounded by water. There are thousands of islands in oceans, lakes, and rivers all over the world. Some are tiny dots of rock. Others are huge countries. Some have large **populations** and bustling cities. Others are too wild and **remote** for anyone to live on.

There are two main types of islands. These are called continental islands and oceanic islands. Continental islands lie on the edge of a **continent**. They are part of that continent. They form when the sea floods a stretch of coast, cutting off a piece of high ground, which becomes an island.

Oceanic islands are islands far out in the oceans. They are not part of any continent. They are the tops of towering volcanoes that grow up from the ocean floor. Most oceanic islands form between two **plates** of Earth's **crust**. Here, **magma** from deep inside Earth builds volcanoes, which may grow into islands.

Greenland

Lying in the North Atlantic Ocean, Greenland is the largest island in the world. It covers 2,166,086 km² (840,000 sq miles), almost one-third the size of Australia. Greenland is a continental island and is part of the **continent** of North America. The island has a rugged coastline, some 39,330 km (24,430 miles) long.

Most Greenlanders live along the island's warmer, southwest coast.

GREENLAND

LOCATION:
NORTH ATLANTIC OCEAN

AREA:
2,166,086 KM² (840,000 SQ MILES)

ISLAND TYPE:
CONTINENTAL

POPULATION:
56,600

THAT'S AMAZING!
GREENLAND WAS GIVEN ITS NAME BY THE VIKINGS, WHO WANTED TO MAKE IT SOUND LIKE A PLEASANT PLACE TO LIVE.

Greenland

NORTH AMERICA

Atlantic Ocean

Ice island

Greenland has an extremely harsh, cold **climate**. More than 80 percent of the island is covered by a gigantic sheet of ice. The ice is 4 km (2.5 miles) thick in places. It is so heavy that the land underneath it has sunk. Scientists are worried that the ice is melting faster than ever before because of **global warming**. This is causing sea levels to rise, putting low-lying places around the world at risk of flooding.

Glaciers flow from this ice sheet in southern Greenland into the sea.

Madagascar

Madagascar is a continental island. It lies off the southeast coast of Africa in the Indian Ocean. It became separated from the **continent** of Africa about 160 million years ago. It is the fourth-largest island in the world. The island has many different types of landscape, from **tropical rain forests**, to mountains, to hot, dry **plains**.

The Mozambique Channel separates Madagascar from Africa.

Amazing wildlife

Madagascar is famous for its amazing wildlife. Three-quarters of its plants and animals are not found anywhere else on Earth. This is because Madagascar has been separated from other land for so long. Madagascar's best-known animals are lemurs. Today, all the **species** of lemur are under threat. People are destroying their forest homes for timber and to make space for farmland.

MADAGASCAR

LOCATION:
INDIAN OCEAN

AREA:
581,540 KM²
(224,533 SQ MILES)

ISLAND TYPE:
CONTINENTAL

POPULATION:
20,042,552

THAT'S AMAZING!
MADAGASCAR IS SOMETIMES CALLED THE "RED ISLAND" BECAUSE OF THE BRIGHT RED COLOR OF ITS SOIL.

AFRICA

Atlantic Ocean

Indian Ocean

Madagascar

Ring-tailed lemurs live in the dry forests of Madagascar.

Hawaii

The island of Hawaii lies in the Pacific Ocean. Hawaii is the biggest island in the Hawaiian Island chain. The chain is made up of eight main islands and around 130 smaller ones.

This is a view of the islands that make up the Hawaiian Island chain.

HAWAII

LOCATION:
PACIFIC OCEAN

AREA:
10,432 KM^2 (4,028 SQ MILES)

ISLAND TYPE:
OCEANIC

POPULATION:
171,000

THAT'S AMAZING!
A NEW HAWAIIAN ISLAND, CALLED LOIHI, IS GROWING ABOVE THE HOT SPOT. IT IS ALREADY 3 KM (1.8 MILES) TALL.

NORTH AMERICA

Pacific Ocean

Atlantic Ocean

Hawaii

Kilauea volcano erupts on the island of Hawaii.

Hot-spot volcanoes

The Hawaiian Islands are oceanic islands that form over a **hot spot** in Earth's **crust**. At a hot spot, **magma** breaks through the seabed and builds a volcano, which grows into an island. The hot spot never moves, but the seabed above it drifts slowly across it. As it does so, the magma breaks new holes in the seabed to form new volcanoes. Over millions of years, a line of hot-spot volcanoes forms a chain of islands.

Sumatra

Sumatra is one of about 17,000 islands in the **archipelago** of Indonesia. An archipelago is a chain of islands. Indonesia is the world's largest archipelago, stretching for more than 5,000 km (3,106 miles) from one end to the other.

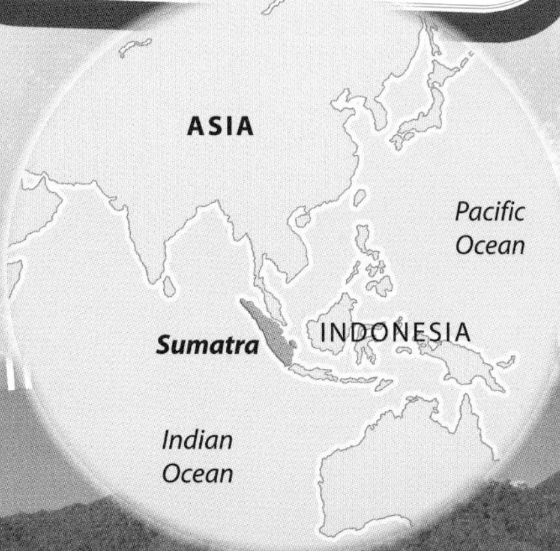

The Barisan Mountains are a chain of volcanoes that run down the west side of Sumatra.

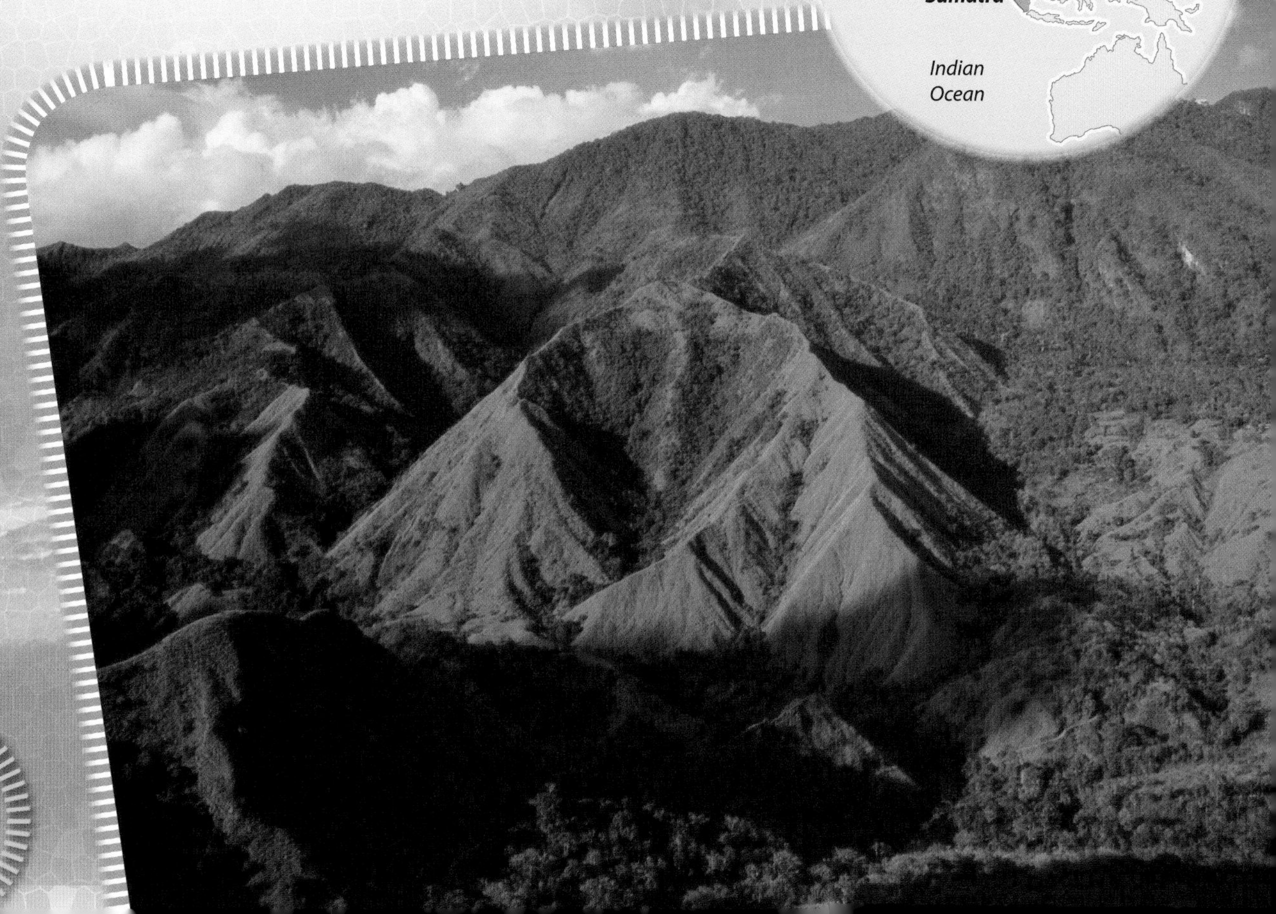

ASIA

Pacific Ocean

Sumatra INDONESIA

Indian Ocean

Giant flower

The rafflesia grows in the rain forests of Sumatra. It is the largest flower in the world and measures about 1 meter (3.2 feet) across. The flower looks and smells like rotten meat to attract flies for **pollination**.

The rafflesia grows inside the roots of rain forest vines.

Island landscape

Sumatra lies across the **equator** and has a **tropical climate**. Most of the island used to be covered in tropical **rain forest**. Large areas have now been cut down for timber and to clear space for farms and **palm-oil plantations**. This has put animals, such as orangutans, in danger of becoming **extinct**.

Rangiroa

Rangiroa lies in the South Pacific Ocean and is one of the world's largest coral atolls (see box, below). Rangiroa is not one island. It is actually a group of about 250 tiny, low-lying coral islands, surrounding a huge, deep blue **lagoon**.

This is part of the coral atoll of Rangiroa, shown from the air.

Coral atolls

A coral atoll forms when a ring of **coral reefs** grows around a volcanic island. Over millions of years, the volcano starts to wear away, leaving an atoll behind.

14

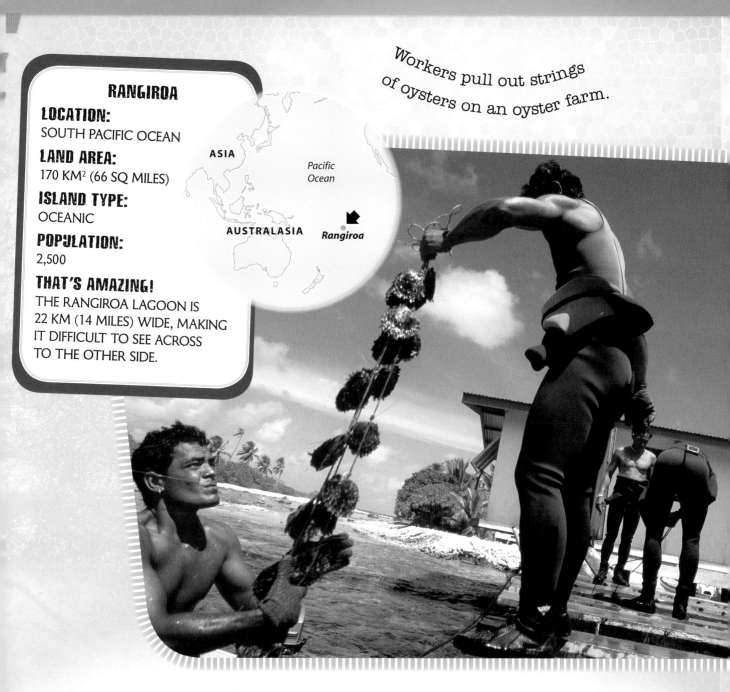

RANGIROA

LOCATION:
SOUTH PACIFIC OCEAN

LAND AREA:
170 KM^2 (66 SQ MILES)

ISLAND TYPE:
OCEANIC

POPULATION:
2,500

THAT'S AMAZING!
THE RANGIROA LAGOON IS 22 KM (14 MILES) WIDE, MAKING IT DIFFICULT TO SEE ACROSS TO THE OTHER SIDE.

ASIA

Pacific Ocean

AUSTRALASIA

Rangiroa

Island lifestyle

Around 2,500 people live on Rangiroa, mostly in two villages. They mainly earn their living from tourism. Tourists visit the island to enjoy the white coral beaches and to snorkel and scuba dive in the lagoon. The islanders also farm oysters in the lagoon. The oysters produce valuable black pearls, which are made into jewelry.

Great Britain

Great Britain is a large island in the Atlantic Ocean, lying to the northwest of mainland Europe. It is the biggest island in Europe. Great Britain is divided into three countries: England, Scotland, and Wales. Great Britain, Ireland, and hundreds of smaller islands off the coast make up the group of islands known as the British Isles.

GREAT BRITAIN

LOCATION:
ATLANTIC OCEAN

AREA:
209,330 KM² (80,822 SQ MILES)

ISLAND TYPE:
CONTINENTAL

POPULATION:
60,975,000

THAT'S AMAZING!
GREAT BRITAIN HAS THE THIRD-LARGEST **POPULATION** OF ANY ISLAND ON EARTH.

Great Britain

EUROPE

Atlantic Ocean

The Shetland Isles lie off the coast of Great Britain.

Island making

One million years ago, a huge sheet of ice covered much of Europe. At that time, Great Britain was joined to Europe. About 10,000 years ago, the ice sheet melted, causing the sea level to rise. This formed the English Channel, which now separates Great Britain from mainland Europe. Movements of Earth's **crust** also meant that sections of the land fell below sea level.

The English Channel separates Great Britain from mainland Europe.

Iceland

Iceland sits on top of a chain of volcanoes that runs down the middle of the Atlantic Ocean. The chain is called the Mid-Atlantic Ridge and is where two **plates** of Earth's **crust** are moving apart. **Magma** rises up to fill the gap and build volcanoes.

New island

In 1963 smoke and steam rose from the sea off the south coast of Iceland. It was a volcano erupting along the Mid-Atlantic Ridge. The volcano created a new island, called Surtsey.

Part of the Mid-Atlantic Ridge can be seen near Reykjavik in Iceland.

ICELAND

LOCATION:
ATLANTIC OCEAN

AREA:
103,000 KM²
(40,000 SQ MILES)

ISLAND TYPE:
OCEANIC

POPULATION:
316,252

THAT'S AMAZING!
AS THE MID-ATLANTIC RIDGE
CONTINUES TO SPREAD, THE
TWO HALVES OF ICELAND ARE
SLOWLY MOVING APART.

Iceland

EUROPE

Atlantic
Ocean

Geysers in Iceland can
erupt to a great height.

Heat from the ground

Volcanoes and **geysers** are
common in Iceland. This
means that there is a lot
of hot rock near the surface
of the ground. Cold water
is pumped into the ground
and heated up by the
rock. Then it is piped into
people's homes. Steam
from the hot water is used
to make electricity.

Galapagos Islands

The Galapagos Islands lie in the Pacific Ocean, off the west coast of South America. There are 13 main islands and several smaller ones. Isabela is the largest island. The islands are volcanic. They sit between three **plates** of Earth's **crust** and on top of a **hot spot**.

Charles Darwin

British scientist Charles Darwin visited the Galapagos Islands in 1835. He noticed that the islands' 13 **species** of finch (a type of bird) had different beak shapes for eating different foods. This showed him that animals develop different features for surviving in different places.

Ecuador Volcano is one of six volcanoes that form Isabela Island.

Island wildlife

Many Galapagos animals, including Galapagos giant tortoises and marine iguanas, live nowhere else on Earth. Today, these unique animals are under threat from goats, cattle, and cats brought over to the islands by settlers.

GALAPAGOS ISLANDS

LOCATION:
PACIFIC OCEAN

AREA:
8,000 KM² (3,089 SQ MILES)

ISLAND TYPE:
OCEANIC

POPULATION:
20,000

THAT'S AMAZING!
THE NAME "GALAPAGOS" COMES FROM THE SPANISH WORD FOR "SADDLE." SOME OF THE ISLANDS' TORTOISES HAD SHELLS THAT LOOKED LIKE OLD SADDLES.

Galapagos Islands

SOUTH AMERICA

Atlantic Ocean

Pacific Ocean

The Galapagos Islands were named after the Galapagos Tortoise. These amazing animals can live for over 100 years!

Honshu

Honshu is the biggest island in the country of Japan. Japan is an **archipelago** of more than 3,000 islands in the Pacific Ocean. The largest islands are Honshu, Hokkaido, Kyushu, and Shikoku. Honshu makes up over half of Japan.

The Ryukyu Islands lie at the southern end of Japan.

HONSHU

LOCATION:
PACIFIC OCEAN

AREA:
230,500 KM^2 (89,000 SQ MILES)

ISLAND TYPE:
OCEANIC

POPULATION:
102,318,000

THAT'S AMAZING!
THE ISLANDS OF HONSHU AND SHIKOKU ARE LINKED BY THE AKASHI-KAIKYO AND OHNARUTO BRIDGES. THE AKASHI-KAIKYO IS THE WORLD'S LONGEST SUSPENSION BRIDGE.

ASIA Honshu

Pacific Ocean

Living space

There is little flat land on Honshu. About three-quarters of the island is covered in mountains or thick forests. This leaves less than a quarter for farming and building. Most people live along the coast, where the towns and cities get very crowded. Honshu has the second-largest **population** of any island. Only Java in southeast Asia has a higher population.

Earthquakes

Hundreds of earthquakes hit Japan each year. This is because Japan sits at the border of three of Earth's **plates**. Earthquakes happen when these plates push and slide against one another.

Tokyo, on Honshu, is Japan's capital and one of the world's most crowded cities.

South Georgia

South Georgia is a bleak and **remote** island in the Southern Ocean. Several other small islands lie off its coast. South Georgia rises steeply from the sea. It has many high mountains, which are covered with ice and snow all year round.

Pairs of King penguins breed on the ice-covered ground of South Georgia.

SOUTH GEORGIA

LOCATION:
SOUTHERN OCEAN

AREA:
3,903 KM² (1,507 SQ MILES)

ISLAND TYPE:
OCEANIC

POPULATION:
0

THAT'S AMAZING!
THE FIRST PERSON TO SEE SOUTH GEORGIA WAS A TRADER FROM LONDON IN 1675. HE CALLED IT "ROCHE ISLAND" (ROCK ISLAND).

SOUTH AMERICA

South Georgia

Southern Ocean

ANTARCTICA

Whaling stations

No one lives on South Georgia permanently, although it is visited by scientists. But, in the early 20th century, it was an important center for whaling. Hundreds of thousands of whales were killed for their **blubber** and meat. Seven whaling stations were built on the island's north coast. Many whales, such as blue, fin, and humpback whales, were nearly wiped out.

Whaling on South Georgia ended in the 1960s. In the 1970s, an international agreement was drawn up to protect the Southern Ocean's whales.

This is the abandoned whaling station of Grytviken, on the west coast of South Georgia.

Islands in Danger

All over the world, islands are in danger. The Maldives are a group of low-lying islands in the Indian Ocean. On average, the islands are only about 1.5 meters (4.9 feet) above sea level. People are now worried that **global warming** could cause the world's ice sheets and **glaciers** to melt. If this happens, the sea level would rise, and the Maldives could become the first islands to disappear beneath the waves.

Low-lying islands like the Maldives are at risk of disappearing if sea levels rise.

These people are clearing litter from a turtle nesting beach in Greece.

Many islands have beautiful beaches and stunning scenery. This makes them popular places for vacations. But building new hotels for tourists causes problems, such as **pollution** and water shortages. It also destroys animals' **habitats**. Sea turtles, for example, lay their eggs on beaches. But these nesting sites are being spoiled by visiting tourists.

Today, conservation groups are working hard to save the world's islands. Some islands, such as the Galapagos Islands (see pages 20–21), have been turned into national parks to protect their amazing wildlife. Only a limited number of tourists are allowed to visit the islands. They can only go there with an experienced, local guide.

Island Facts and Figures

There are thousands of islands, in every ocean. Some islands lie off the edges of **continents** and were once joined to the mainland. Others are the tops of volcanoes, rising from the seabed. Which island do you think is the most amazing?

This map of the world shows all the islands described in this book. "Australasia" describes Australia, New Zealand, and a series of nearby islands in the Pacific Ocean.

Arctic Ocean

Greenland

Iceland

ASIA

Great Britain

NORTH AMERICA

EUROPE

Honshu

Atlantic Ocean

Hawaii

AFRICA

Pacific Ocean

Galapagos Islands

SOUTH AMERICA

Sumatra

INDONESIA

Indian Ocean

AUSTRALASIA

Rangiroa

Madagascar

Pacific Ocean

South Georgia

Southern Ocean

ANTARCTICA

GREENLAND

AREA:
2,166,086 KM² (840,000 SQ MILES)

ISLAND TYPE:
CONTINENTAL

POPULATION:
56,600

MADAGASCAR

AREA:
581,540 KM² (224,533 SQ MILES)

ISLAND TYPE:
CONTINENTAL

POPULATION:
20,042,552

HAWAII

AREA:
10,432 KM² (4,028 SQ MILES)

ISLAND TYPE:
OCEANIC

POPULATION:
171,000

SUMATRA

AREA:
470,000 KM² (181,468 SQ MILES)

ISLAND TYPE:
OCEANIC

POPULATION:
45,000,000

RANGIROA

LAND AREA:
170 KM² (66 SQ MILES)

ISLAND TYPE:
OCEANIC

POPULATION:
2,500

GREAT BRITAIN

AREA:
209,330 KM² (80,822 SQ MILES)

ISLAND TYPE:
CONTINENTAL

POPULATION:
60,975,000

ICELAND

AREA:
103,000 KM² (40,000 SQ MILES)

ISLAND TYPE:
OCEANIC

POPULATION:
316,252

GALAPAGOS ISLANDS

AREA:
8,000 KM² (3,089 SQ MILES)

ISLAND TYPE:
OCEANIC

POPULATION:
20,000

HONSHU

AREA:
230,500 KM² (89,000 SQ MILES)

ISLAND TYPE:
OCEANIC

POPULATION:
102,318,000

SOUTH GEORGIA

AREA:
3,903 KM² (1,507 SQ MILES)

ISLAND TYPE:
OCEANIC

POPULATION:
0

Find Out More

Books to read

Chambers, Catherine, and Nicholas Lapthorn. *Mapping Earthforms: Islands*. Chicago: Heinemann Library, 2008.

Ganeri, Anita. *Horrible Geography: Wild Islands*. New York: Scholastic, 2004.

Morris, Neil. *Landscapes and People: Earth's Changing Islands*. Chicago: Raintree, 2004.

Websites

Island Directory
http://islands.unep.ch/isldir
This website offers a directory of thousands of islands, listing them by size, **population**, type, and so on.

World Atlas
www.worldatlas.com
This website lists all of the world's islands, with facts, maps, and figures about many of them.

Hawaii's Bishop Museum
www.bishopmuseum.org/research/cultstud/kaho/facts.htm
Learn more facts about the Hawaiian Islands at the website.

Glossary

archipelago large group of islands

blubber fat of a sea mammal, such as a seal

climate overall weather patterns on Earth, or in a part of the world

continent continuous landmass. There are seven continents on Earth.

coral reef large underwater structure made of layers of coral built over many years

crust outer, rocky surface of Earth

equator imaginary line around the middle of Earth

extinct when a species has died out and no longer exists

geyser tall spring of scalding steam and hot water

glacier river of ice that flows slowly down a mountain

global warming gradual warming of Earth

habitat where a plant or animal lives

hot spot weak area in Earth's crust where volcanoes can form

lagoon area of water cut off from the sea by a coral reef

magma hot, molten (liquid) rock that lies underneath Earth's solid crust

palm-oil oil from the fruit of some types of palms

plain flat stretch of land, often without many trees

plantation very large farm where crops such as oil palms are grown

plate huge section of Earth's crust. The crust is broken into several plates.

pollination when pollen is carried from one plant to another in order to make seeds that will grow into new plants

pollution waste and dirt that can damage Earth

population number of people living in a particular place

rain forest thick forest growing around the equator where the climate is hot and wet

remote located in a far-off or distant place

species particular type of living thing

tropical places around the equator, which are hot and wet all year round

Index